Price Per Sq. Ft. is Lying to You

Price Per Sq. Ft. is Lying to You

Rahul Gupta

First Printing, 2026

CONTENTS

DEDICATION

This book is dedicated to every family that trusted us with their dreams, savings, and future. Your belief shaped our responsibility and our standards.

PREFACE

Buying a property is one of the biggest financial and emotional decisions of life. Yet, most buyers are guided by half-truths, sales pitches, and surface-level comparisons. This book was written to slow you down, sharpen your thinking, and help you make decisions you will feel proud of years from now.

ACKNOWLEDGEMENT

This book would not have been possible without the people who stood beside me long before it was written — quietly, consistently, and selflessly.

First and foremost, my deepest gratitude goes to my wife, Tanvi. Your patience, belief, and emotional strength have been my anchor through every demanding phase of this journey. You carried the weight of long days, uncertain moments, and silent sacrifices with grace — often without asking for recognition. This book carries your support in every page.

To my son, Akshat — you are my greatest inspiration.

You remind me why integrity, responsibility, and long-term thinking truly matter. Everything I build today is with the hope that tomorrow you inherit not just assets, but values.

I owe everything to my parents, RD Gupta and Laxmi Gupta

Your values laid the foundation long before the first project or transaction. You taught me the importance of honesty, humility, and standing by one's word — lessons that continue to guide every decision I make. This book is as much a reflection of your upbringing as it is of my experience.

To my sister, Kamini, thank you for your unwavering encouragement and belief. Your support, understanding, and presence have been a constant source of strength throughout this journey.

I would also like to sincerely thank my company team, who work tirelessly behind the scenes. Your dedication, professionalism, and commitment to doing things the right way make everything we promise possible. This book represents not just my voice, but the collective effort and integrity of an entire team.

Finally, to every client who trusted us with their dreams, savings, and future — thank you. Your belief is the responsibility we carry every day.

This book is not just a professional milestone.

It is a reflection of family, values, trust, and the people who made the journey meaningful.

Love & Gratitude
Rahul Gupta, CEO of Neoteric Properties

KNOW YOUR AUTHOR

I entered real estate during a market crash — not a boom. Sleepless nights, rebuilding trust, and carrying forward a family legacy shaped my approach to this business.

Over the last 40 years, we have delivered 65+ projects and served 10,000+ clients across 27 countries. Landmark projects like Neoteric NG Grande, once Madhya Pradesh's tallest building, redefined our commitment to trust, quality, and timely delivery.

My values remain simple: Integrity, Empathy, and Family Values.

1 Introduction

This is not a book about buying cheap property. This is a book about buying right. Over four decades in real estate, I've seen buyers succeed, struggle, and regret — often for reasons that had nothing to do with market conditions and everything to do with decision-making. These pages will help you avoid common traps and build clarity before commitment.

Why this book?

This book exists because too many buyers:

- Focus on price instead of value
- Rush decisions under pressure
- Ignore trust and long-term livability

The goal is simple: help you become a confident buyer, not a hopeful one.

2

The Square-Foot Fallacy

Why Price Per Sq. Ft. Is the Most Expensive Mistake Most Buyers Make?

"The bitterness of poor quality remains long after the sweetness of low price is forgotten."- ***Benjamin Franklin***

For most property buyers, the first — and sometimes only — question is:

"What is the price per square foot?"

It sounds logical. Simple. Comparable. But in reality, this single metric has caused more regret, stress, and financial loss than almost any other mistake in real estate. After working with over 10,000 clients across 27 countries, I can say this with confidence:

Price per sq. ft. is not a decision tool — it's a distraction.

Why Buyers Obsess Over Price Per Sq. Ft. Because it feels safe. When buyers compare two properties, one at ₹4,000/sq. ft. and another at ₹5,500/sq. ft., the cheaper one automatically feels like a better deal. But what most buyers don't realize is that price per sq. ft. ignores 70% of the real cost of ownership. Let's look at a simple example. Two flats. Same size. Same city.

- Project A: Lower price per sq. ft.
  - Delayed possession by 3 years
  - Poor construction quality
  - No proper maintenance
  - Weak resale demand

- Project B: Higher price per sq. ft.
  - On-time delivery
  - Reputed developer
  - Strong community & amenities
  - Higher rental & resale value

On paper, Project A looks cheaper. In real life, Project B makes you wealthier — financially and mentally.

The Hidden Costs Buyers Don't Calculate

When you focus only on price per sq. ft., you miss:

- **Time cost:** Delayed possession means rent + EMI together

- **Stress cost:** Constant follow-ups, uncertainty, legal anxiety
- **Quality cost:** Repairs, seepage, poor fittings after possession
- **Opportunity cost:** Lost appreciation and rental income

Ironically, the "cheapest" property often becomes the most expensive decision over 5–10 years.

What Smart Buyers Do Differently

Experienced buyers and professionals don't ask, "Is this cheap?" They ask:

- Will I get possession on time?
- Can I trust this developer with my life savings?
- Will this property still be desirable after 10 years?
- Does this home support my lifestyle and family values?

They evaluate value per square foot, not price.

The Real Question You Should Ask

Instead of: "What is the price per sq. ft.?" Ask:
"What am I truly paying for — and what am I risking?"

When buyers shift this mindset, decisions become clearer, calmer, and more confident.

Worksheet: Are You Overpaying or Underthinking?

Answer honestly. Give yourself 1 point for every "YES."

1. Am I choosing this property mainly because it's cheaper per sq. ft.?
2. Do I fully trust the developer's past delivery record?
3. Have I checked possession timelines realistically?
4. Do I understand maintenance quality and long-term costs?
5. Will this property be desirable for resale or rent after 10 years?
6. Does this project match my lifestyle and family needs?
7. Have I evaluated the neighborhood, not just the flat?
8. Am I clear about legal paperwork and approvals?
9. Would I buy this property even if prices didn't rise for 5 years?
10. Do I feel peaceful — not pressured — about this decision?

Your Score & What It Means

- **8–10 YES:** You're thinking like a smart, long-term buyer

- **5–7 YES:** You need a deeper evaluation before committing
- **Below 5 YES:** You are at high risk of making a costly mistake.

Conclusion:

If price per sq. ft. is your main filter, pause. Smart real estate decisions are built on trust, timing, and total value — not just numbers.

3

Strategic Inquiry

The One Question Smart Buyers Ask Before Even Seeing the Property

"Wise people ask better questions, not faster answers."
- Anonymous

Most buyers believe the real decision begins after visiting a site. Smart buyers know the truth:

The decision starts before you even step into the property.

In fact, experienced buyers ask one powerful question early — and it saves them years of stress, money, and regret.

The Question That Changes Everything

Before site visits, floor plans, or discounts, smart buyers ask:

"Can this developer deliver what they are promising — on time and without excuses?"

This single question filters out 70% of bad deals immediately

Yet most buyers skip it. Instead, they ask:

- "Is there a discount?"
- "What's the price per sq. ft.?"
- "How soon can I book?"

These are transaction questions, not trust questions.

Why This Question Matters So Much

Real estate is not an instant product.

You don't buy and receive it the next day. You commit:

- Your savings
- Your EMIs
- Your family's future
- Your mental peace for years.

If the developer fails, everything suffers — timelines, finances, relationships, and trust. Over the last 40 years, we've seen this repeatedly:

Good projects fail not because of bad design, but because of poor delivery discipline.

How Smart Buyers Find the Real Answer

Developers will always say:

"Sir, the project is on track."

Smart buyers dig deeper. They check:

- Past projects — not promises
- Actual possession dates — not planned ones
- Quality after 5–10 years — not showroom finishes
- How the developer handled tough market phases

A developer who delivered during slowdowns and crashes is far more reliable than one who thrived only in booms.

A Real-Life Pattern We've Observed

Buyers who skip this question usually face:

- Delayed possession
- Constant follow-ups
- Design compromises
- Legal confusion
- Emotional exhaustion

Buyers who ask it early experience:

- Predictable timelines
- Transparent communication

- Stable communities
- Strong resale demand

The difference isn't luck. It's due diligence.

Why Most Buyers Avoid Asking This

Because it's uncomfortable.

Asking tough questions feels awkward. Buyers worry about appearing difficult or missing out on a "deal."

But remember:

A confident developer welcomes questions.
A weak one avoids them.

Your New Buying Filter

Before seeing any property, ask:

- Who has trusted this developer before me?
- What did they experience after booking?
- Would I feel safe investing my family's savings here?

If the answers aren't clear — don't move forward.

Worksheet: Are You Asking the Right Question?

Give yourself 1 point for every "YES."

1. Have I researched the developer's past projects?
2. Do I know their actual possession track record?
3. Have I spoken to existing customers, not just sales teams?
4. Has the developer delivered during tough market phases?
5. Do they communicate clearly, without over-promising?
6. Are approvals and documentation transparent?
7. Do I feel confident asking tough questions here?
8. Is their reputation strong beyond advertisements?
9. Would I trust this developer with my own family's investment?
10. Am I choosing based on trust, not urgency?

Your Score & Meaning

- **8–10 YES:** You're filtering like a professional buyer
- **5–7 YES:** Pause and investigate deeper
- **Below 5 YES**: High risk — rethink before proceeding

Conclusion:

The smartest buyers don't rush to see properties. They first confirm who they are buying from.

4

The Delay Model

Delayed Possession: Accident or Hidden Business Model?

"Time is the most expensive currency — once lost, it can never be earned back." - ***Anonymous***

Ask any property buyer about their biggest fear, and you'll hear the same answer again and again:

"Will I actually get possession on time?"

Delayed possession is so common that many buyers have begun accepting it as "normal." But here's a hard truth from 40 years in real estate:

Most possession delays are not accidents. They are predictable — and often avoidable.

Why Delays Hurt More Than Buyers Realize

When possession is delayed, the loss isn't just emotional — it's financial and personal. Buyers usually face:

- Double burden: Rent + EMI together
- Lifestyle disruption: Plans postponed indefinitely
- Mental stress: Endless follow-ups and excuses
- Lost opportunities: Appreciation and rental income vanish

A 2-year delay can silently cost lakhs — sometimes more than the price difference buyers initially negotiated.

The Uncomfortable Reality

Some developers launch projects before they are truly ready. They depend on:

- Advance bookings to fund construction
- Future sales to finish current promises
- Market optimism instead of execution discipline

When markets slow or approvals stall, buyers pay the price — not the developer. This is why smart buyers don't ask "What is the possession date?" They ask:

"What makes you confident you can deliver on that date?"

How Smart Buyers Spot Delay Risks Early

Before booking, experienced buyers check:

- Has this developer completed similar projects before?
- Did they deliver on time, not just eventually?
- Is construction progress visible — or only advertised?
- Are approvals already in place or "under process"?

A developer with approvals, funding clarity, and execution experience rarely delays possession.

A Pattern We've Seen Repeatedly

Projects that delay usually show early warning signs:

- Heavy discounts before foundation work
- Vague timelines like "expected possession"
- Aggressive marketing but slow site progress
- Poor communication once bookings increase

Projects that deliver on time show discipline:

- Conservative timelines
- Transparent updates
- Fewer promises, stronger execution

The Buyer's Mindset Shift.

Instead of hoping for the best, ask yourself:

- Can I afford a 2–3 year delay financially and emotionally?
- Does this developer respect timelines as much as sales?
- Am I trusting words — or verified track record?

Remember:

Possession delay is not a surprise. It's usually a warning ignored.

Worksheet: Are You at Risk of Delayed Possession?

Give yourself 1 point for every "YES."

1. Has the developer delivered previous projects on time?
2. Are major approvals already secured?
3. Is construction progress visible and consistent?
4. Are possession dates realistic, not overly optimistic?
5. Is funding clear without overdependence on bookings?
6. Do updates come regularly without chasing?
7. Are timelines documented in agreements?
8. Does the developer avoid vague commitments?
9. Have I factored in worst-case delay scenarios?

10. Do I feel confident this project will finish even in slow markets?

Your Score & Meaning

- **8–10 YES:** Low risk, well-evaluated decision
- **5–7 YES:** Caution — investigate further
- **Below 5 YES:** High risk of delay

Conclusion:

Buying property is not about optimism — it's about preparedness. Choose developers who respect time as much as money.

5

The Safety Net

Paperwork Isn't Paperwork — It's Your Safety Net

"Trust is good. Documentation is better." - ***Real Estate Wisdom***

For many buyers, paperwork is the most ignored part of buying a property. It feels boring, confusing, and technical — something to "get done" quickly. But after four decades in real estate, here's a simple truth:

Paperwork doesn't create problems. Ignoring it does.

Why Buyers Fear Paperwork

Most buyers avoid documents because:

- Legal language feels intimidating
- Everyone says, "Don't worry, it's standard"

- They trust the brand or recommendation blindly

Unfortunately, this is where mistakes quietly begin.

A beautiful home with weak paperwork is not an asset — it's a liability.

What Paperwork Really Protects You From

Strong documentation protects buyers from:

- Ownership disputes
- Delayed possession without compensation
- Hidden charges and surprise clauses
- Legal complications during resale or inheritance

When paperwork is clear, your investment remains stress-free for decades.

Common Documentation Traps Buyers Fall Into

We've seen buyers struggle later because:

- Agreements lacked clear possession timelines
- Penalty clauses applied only to buyers, not developers
- Approvals were "applied for" but not received
- Verbal promises never made it into writing

Remember:

If it's not written, it doesn't exist

What Smart Buyers Insist On

Experienced buyers don't rush paperwork. They confirm:

- Title clarity and land ownership
- Approved layout and building permissions
- Clearly mentioned possession dates
- Defined penalty clauses for delays
- Transparent maintenance and handover terms

They understand that paperwork is not about distrust — it's about protection.

A Simple Rule to Follow

If a developer says: "This clause is never used." Ask: "Then why is it there?"

Confidence in paperwork reflects confidence in delivery.

Your Long-Term Safety

Your property may change hands — through resale, inheritance, or gifting.

Clean paperwork ensures:

- Smooth resale
- Higher valuation
- Zero legal stress for your family

In real estate, paperwork doesn't slow decisions. It secures them.

Worksheet: How Strong Is Your Safety Net?

Give yourself **1 point for every "YES."**

1. Have I verified clear land title and ownership?
2. Are all major approvals already in place?
3. Is possession date clearly mentioned in writing?
4. Are delay penalties clearly defined for the developer?
5. Are payment schedules linked to construction progress?
6. Are verbal promises documented in agreements?
7. Is maintenance cost transparency provided?
8. Have I taken independent legal advice if needed?
9. Do documents support easy resale in future?
10. Would I feel comfortable explaining this paperwork to my family?

Your Score & Meaning

- **8–10 YES**: Strong legal foundation
- **5–7 YES:** Needs careful review
- **Below 5 YES:** High legal risk

Conclusion:

A property backed by solid paperwork is peace of mind — today and tomorrow.

6

The Five-Year Horizon

ROI vs Reality: What Returns Actually Look Like After 5 Years

*"An investment that looks good on paper must survive real life." - **Anonymous***

Real estate conversations often begin with one word: ROI. Buyers are shown attractive numbers — projected appreciation, expected rentals, future value charts.

But very few stop to ask:

"What will this investment actually look like after 5 years?"

After guiding thousands of investors, one lesson stands out:

Real estate returns are rarely instant — and never uniform.

Why ROI Is Often Misunderstood

Most ROI discussions ignore:

- Vacant periods without rental income
- Maintenance and society costs
- Market cycles and slowdowns
- Liquidity challenges during resale

A property may look profitable in brochures but perform very differently in reality.

A Simple 5-Year Reality Check

Let's say you buy a property expecting:

- 10–12% annual appreciation
- Immediate rental income

But in real life:

- Possession delays reduce income years
- Rentals take time to stabilize
- Maintenance increases yearly
- Market appreciation moves in cycles

Suddenly, the "high ROI" looks far more modest — unless the property was chosen wisely.

What Actually Drives Long-Term Returns

In reality, strong ROI comes from:

- Location quality, not just location name
- Developer reputation, not just project size
- Livability, which attracts long-term tenants
- Maintenance standards, which protect value

A well-managed project with moderate appreciation often outperforms a flashy project with poor fundamentals.

The Emotional Side of Returns

Investors underestimate emotional ROI:

- Peace of mind
- Predictable income
- Stress-free ownership

An investment that keeps you anxious is costing you more than money.

The Smarter Way to Evaluate ROI

Instead of asking: "How much will this grow?" Ask:

- Will this property stay desirable?
- Can I hold it comfortably for 5–10 years?

- Will tenants want to live here long-term?
- Can I exit easily if needed?

Returns follow confidence — not hype

Worksheet: Is Your ROI Expectation Realistic?

Give yourself **1 point for every "YES."**

1. Have I calculated net returns, not just projected ones?
2. Have I considered possession and vacancy timelines?
3. Do maintenance costs make sense long-term?
4. Is rental demand strong and sustainable?
5. Is the developer known for value appreciation?
6. Can I hold this property comfortably for 5+ years?
7. Is resale demand likely even in slow markets?
8. Does this investment align with my financial goals?
9. Am I comfortable with conservative return assumptions?
10. Would I still buy this property if returns were moderate?

Your Score & Meaning

- **8–10 YES:** Balanced and realistic investor mindset
- **5–7 YES:** Revisit assumptions
- **Below 5 YES:** High risk of disappointment

Conclusion:

True ROI rewards patience, planning, and quality decisions

7

The Primacy of Context

Why Neighborhood Choice Matters More Than Flat Size

"You don't just buy a home. You buy a way of life."
- ***Anonymous***

Many buyers focus intensely on carpet area, balcony size, or number of rooms. But years later, what truly defines happiness — and property value — is something else entirely:

The neighborhood you live in.

A slightly smaller home in the right neighborhood often delivers far more satisfaction than a bigger home in the wrong one.

Why Size Feels Important Initially

When buyers compare homes, size is visible and measurable. Neighborhood quality feels abstract — until you live there.

But over time, daily life reveals the truth.

What Neighborhood Really Means

A neighborhood is not just about location on a map. It includes:

- People you live around
- Noise levels and cleanliness
- Safety and security
- Schools, hospitals, and daily conveniences
- Community culture and maintenance standards

These factors shape your routine, peace of mind, and long-term happiness.

How Neighborhood Impacts Value

Properties in strong neighborhoods:

- Appreciate more steadily
- Attract better tenants
- Sell faster during resale
- Age gracefully over time

Weak neighborhoods struggle— regardless of flat size or interior upgrades.

A Simple Example

Two properties:

- **Flat A:** Larger size, poor surroundings, low maintenance.
- **Flat B:** Slightly smaller, strong community, disciplined upkeep

After 5–7 years:

Flat B commands higher resale and rental demand — almost every time.

The Professional Buyer's Lens

Smart buyers ask:

- Who will my neighbors be?
- Is this a community I'll be proud of?
- Will my family feel safe and comfortable here?
- Will this area improve or deteriorate over time?

They know that homes age — neighborhoods evolve.

Your Lifestyle Check

A good neighborhood reduces stress:

- Children play safely
- Social interactions feel comfortable
- Property upkeep remains consistent

That emotional return compounds every day.

Worksheet: Is the Neighborhood Right for You?

Give yourself **1 point for every "YES."**

1. Do I feel comfortable with the surrounding community?
2. Is safety visibly prioritized?
3. Are daily needs easily accessible?
4. Is cleanliness and maintenance consistent?
5. Do I see long-term development potential?
6. Would I be proud to invite guests here?
7. Is this a good environment for my family?
8. Would tenants prefer this location?
9. Does the neighborhood support resale demand?
10. Do I feel peaceful imagining life here?

Your Score & Meaning

- **8–10 YES:** Strong lifestyle and investment choice
- **5–7 YES:** Needs deeper evaluation
- **Below 5 YES:** High risk of dissatisfaction

Conclusion:

Square feet define space. Neighborhood defines life.

8

The Trust Foundation

Trust Is Built Before First Payment, Not After Possession

"In real estate, trust is not promised — it is proven." - ***Anonymous***

Most buyers believe trust is something that develops after possession.

They assume, "Once I get my flat, everything will be fine." But after 40 years in real estate, here's a truth few admit:

If trust is weak before booking, possession won't fix it.

Trust is either present at the start — or missing altogether.

Why Trust Is the Real Currency in Real Estate

Real estate is unlike buying a car or a gadget. You don't exchange money and walk away.

You commit:

- Large savings
- Long-term EMIs
- Your family's future
- Your mental peace for years

Once the first payment is made, buyers often feel **locked in** — emotionally and financially.

That's why trust must be evaluated **before dependence begins**.

How Genuine Trust Reveals Itself Early

Trust is not created through branding or brochures. It shows up quietly in behavior.

A trustworthy developer:

- Gives clear answers, even when they're uncomfortable
- Explains risks, not just rewards
- Sets realistic expectations, not inflated ones
- Is comfortable when buyers slow down to think

Confidence without pressure is a strong signal of integrity.

The Difference Between Sales Confidence and Trust

Sales confidence sounds like:

"Sir, everything is approved."

"Sir, don't worry, this is standard."

"Sir, prices are increasing tomorrow."

Trust sounds like:

"Let's verify this together."

"Take time to review the documents."

"This project is not right for everyone — and that's okay."

One pushes decisions. The other supports them.

Why Pressure Is the Enemy of Trust

Urgency has its place in life — not in life-altering investments. Pressure tactics often hide:

- Cash flow stress
- Overdependence on bookings
- Weak planning

A developer who pressures you today may avoid you tomorrow when challenges arise.

A Simple Test Most Buyers Never Use

Ask a direct question:

"What could go wrong with this project?"

A trustworthy developer will answer honestly. Avoidance, deflection, or irritation is your answer.

Trust Is Also About How Problems Are Handled

No project is perfect.

Delays, changes, and market shifts happen

Trust is revealed in:

- Communication during uncertainty
- Accountability when things slow down
- Consistency when markets weaken

Promises matter less than response during pressure.

Your Inner Alignment Matters

Beyond documents and discussions, listen to yourself. Ask:

- Do I feel respected here?
- Am I being educated or persuaded?

- Do I feel calm — or rushed?

Your body often senses misalignment before your mind accepts it.

Expanded Worksheet: Measuring Trust Before Commitment

Give yourself **1 point for every "YES."**

1. Are answers transparent, even when inconvenient?
2. Is there encouragement to review and verify documents?
3. Are timelines realistic and conservative?
4. Is urgency created artificially or naturally?
5. Does the developer acknowledge risks openly?
6. Is communication consistent without chasing?
7. Are tough questions welcomed?
8. Are past clients comfortable sharing experiences?
9. Do actions match words consistently?
10. Do I feel respected, not pressured?

Your Score & What It Reveals

- **8–10 YES:** Strong trust foundation
- **5–7 YES:** Mixed signals — proceed carefully
- **Below 5 YES:** Trust gap — pause and reassess

Final Thought

You don't buy real estate with money alone. You buy it with trust.

Choose partners who protect your peace of mind — not just your investment.

9

The Luxury Standard

Luxury Isn't Marble — It's Maintenance, Management & Mindset

*"True luxury is not what shines on day one, but what still works on day one thousand."- **Anonymous***

When buyers hear the word luxury, they imagine Italian marble, designer fittings, and grand entrances.

These features attract attention — but they don't define long-term living.

After decades in real estate, one truth stands clear:

Luxury is experienced every day, not showcased on possession day.

The Illusion of Visible Luxury

Show homes are designed to impress:

- Glossy finishes
- Dramatic lighting
- Perfect staging

But many buyers learn too late that visual luxury fades quickly if the foundation is weak.

Cracked tiles can be replaced. Poor management cannot.

What Real Luxury Feels Like

Real luxury is:

- Elevators that work consistently
- Clean common areas year after year
- Reliable security and power backup
- Quick issue resolution
- Predictable maintenance standards

These are not glamorous — but they define daily comfort.

Why Maintenance Decides Long-Term Value

Well-maintained properties:

- Retain premium perception
- Attract better residents and tenants
- Command higher resale prices
- Age gracefully instead of deteriorating

Poor maintenance turns even premium projects into ordinary ones.

The Role of Professional Management

Strong management ensures:

- Transparent maintenance usage
- Disciplined vendor handling
- Community harmony
- Asset value protection

Luxury without management is temporary. Management without luxury still delivers comfort.

The Mindset Shift Buyers Must Make

Instead of asking: "How does it look?" Ask:

- How will this function after 5 years?
- Who maintains this community?
- What standards are enforced?
- Will quality be protected when novelty fades?

Luxury is a system, not a surface.

Worksheet: Is This Real Luxury or Just Appearance?

Give yourself **1 point for every "YES."**

1. Are maintenance systems clearly defined?
2. Is professional property management involved?
3. Are long-term costs transparent?
4. Do common areas reflect quality upkeep?
5. Is security well-managed, not just installed?
6. Are rules and standards clearly enforced?
7. Will this project age gracefully?
8. Do residents share a quality-first mindset?
9. Is management proactive, not reactive?
10. Does this luxury feel sustainable long-term?

Your Score & Meaning

- **8–10 YES:** True luxury living
- **5–7 YES:** Mixed experience likely
- **Below 5 YES:** Surface-level appeal only

10

The Generational Equity

Buying for Today vs. Buying for the Next Generation

"A home is not just shelter for today — it is security for tomorrow."- ***Anonymous***

Most buyers purchase property thinking about current needs:

- Today's budget
- Today's lifestyle
- Today's space requirements

But experienced buyers think differently. They ask:

"Will this decision still feel right 10–20 years from now?"

The Difference Between Short-Term Comfort and Long-Term Wisdom

Buying for today focuses on:

- Immediate affordability
- Present convenience
- Quick possession

Buying for the next generation considers:

- Location longevity
- Community quality
- Legal clarity
- Resale and inheritance ease

Short-term decisions often require long-term corrections.

Why Generational Wealth Requires Patience

Properties that build generational wealth:

- Are held through market cycles
- Prioritize stability over speculation
- Sit in strong, improving neighborhoods
- Come from reliable developers

They may not feel exciting at purchase — but they feel reassuring over time.

A Common Regret We Hear

Many families say:

“We wish we had chosen quality over size.”

“We should have focused on the neighborhood.”

“We didn’t think about resale or inheritance.”

These regrets surface years later — when options are limited.

What Future-Proof Buyers Consider

Smart buyers think ahead:

- Will my children want to live here?
- Will this property remain relevant?
- Will legal transfer be smooth?
- Will maintenance standards remain high?

A home that grows with your family becomes an asset beyond numbers.

Your Legacy Lens

When you buy property, you don’t just decide for yourself — you decide for your family’s future.

Worksheet: Are You Buying with the Next Generation in Mind?

Give yourself **1 point for every "YES."**

1. Is the location future-ready?
2. Does the community support long-term living?
3. Is paperwork inheritance-friendly?
4. Will this property age well?
5. Is maintenance quality sustainable?
6. Will resale demand remain strong?
7. Is the developer's legacy reliable?
8. Can this asset be comfortably held long-term?
9. Does it align with family values?
10. Will this decision still feel wise in 20 years?

Your Score & Meaning

- **8–10 YES:** Strong generational asset
- **5–7 YES:** Needs long-term rethinking
- **Below 5 YES:** Short-term decision

11

The Decisive Protocol

Final Checklist That Separates Confident Buyers from Regretful Ones

"Confidence comes not from hope, but from preparation."
*- **Anonymous***

By now, you've learned that buying real estate is not about chasing deals or trends. It's about making informed, calm, and future-ready decisions.

This final chapter brings everything together into a single decision framework.

Why Most Regrets Are Preventable

Buyers rarely regret buying real estate. They regret how they bought it.

Common regrets include:

- Rushing due to pressure
- Ignoring early warning signs
- Choosing price over trust
- Focusing on size instead of sustainability

Regret doesn't come from lack of information — it comes from ignoring it.

The Confident Buyer's Mindset

Confident buyers:

- Don't rush
- Ask tough questions
- Think long-term
- Prioritize peace of mind

They understand that a good property decision should reduce stress, not create it.

Your Go / No-Go Framework

Before booking, confident buyers mentally check:

- Trust in the developer
- Clarity of paperwork

- Realistic timelines
- Neighborhood quality
- Long-term livability

Final Worksheet: Are You a Confident Buyer?

Give yourself 1 point for every "YES."

1. Do I trust the developer completely?
2. Is paperwork clear and transparent?
3. Are possession timelines realistic?
4. Is the neighborhood future-ready?
5. Does this property support my lifestyle?
6. Is maintenance sustainably planned?
7. Will this property age gracefully?
8. Can I hold this asset long-term?
9. Do I feel calm about this decision?
10. Would I recommend this project to family?

Your Final Score & Conclusion

- **8–10 YES:** You're a confident, prepared buyer
- **5–7 YES:** Pause and re-evaluate
- **Below 5 YES:** Step back — not ready yet

Final Thought:

The best property decision feels steady, not urgent.

12

Connect With the Author

If you believe real estate should be trustworthy, timely, and transformational, we'd love to connect.

Company: Leaders in Real Estate

Experience: 40+ Years

Clients Served: 10,000+ across 27 countries

Because the right property decision should give you peace — not pressure.

Website of Neoteric Properties

LinkedIn Page of the Author